CLASSIC ART MEMES

When you try to explain to your Dad you've dropped out of college to pursue a career in shadow puppetry.

*When the DJ plays your
tune and you own the floor.*

When you meet your Tinder[TM] date for the first time and you realise it must have been a typo when he said he liked M&S[TM].

*When your man tries to persuade
you that this bout of man flu
is genuinely serious.*

When you turn the TV on at your grandparent's house and the volume is on maximum.

When you've been waiting ages just to be able to ask for the bill.

When you could literally kill your squad for setting you up on this blind date.

*When your mate starts
telling you 'that' story again.*

When you're out on your stag do with the lads and your dad has tagged along.

When you've spread a funny rumour and you hear it being passed around the office.

When you realise series record hasn't been working the whole time you were away on holiday.

When you stand in Waitrose™ and judge everyone who you don't think is posh enough to be in there with you.

*When you are busy jammin'
on your harp and aren't sure
if you heard the doorbell.*

When you run it by your
mate before swiping right.

When you try a little too hard to look good on your Tinder™ profile.

When you check all your pockets,
but can't find your phone.

When she says "you're like a brother to me".

When you thought you would have your usual from the McDonald's™ menu, but something new catches your eye.

When a guy tries to convince you
he's a Trekkie but you're not so sure.

When you overhear people talking about you at work but try to not make it obvious you are listening in.

When the singer keeps stopping band practice to change something.

When he insists on making you listen to his new song just one more time.

When you slip on the steps, but style it out and hope no one noticed.

When your mates are trying to work out who ate what, and you're just happy to split the bill evenly.

*When you're subtly trying
to get someone to ask you
about your new trousers.*

When you regret agreeing to look after your neighbour's cats.

When haters gonna hate.

When you mime to your favourite song like no one's watching.

When you plead to your girl to let the lads sleep in the spare room for just one more night.

When the guy standing next to you on the Tube can't keep control of his elbow.

When you turn it up to 11.

When, for a second, you remember your life before having kids.

When you're struggling to get the key in the door because you're hammered and seeing double.

When the commute
home is just dragging.

*When your flute playing
is underappreciated.*

When you are 5 ft 11" and she says she only dates guys over 6 ft.

When you look to your mates to get you away from the drunk guy, but they are nowhere to be seen.

*When only an expression
sums up your disappointment.*

When you have to do that awkward pose for the press while signing your new football team contract.

When you are bringing the food to the table and your friend announces they've gone vegan.

When you look back and can't believe you were so excited that he offered to take you out dancing.

When you convince the doctor that 'hating Monday mornings' should be a medically recognised condition.

When your parents announce you're getting a new little sister.

When your new girl is just a bit too clingy.

When you go to write something down,
but immediately forget what it was.

When you walk into a house warming party and see 'Live, Laugh, Love' stencilled on the wall.

*When you are hoping to
get noticed at the gym, but
pretend to just be chillin'.*

*When your phone is low on battery,
but the charger is in the other room.*

When you pop outside to grab the milk and the door locks behind you.

When you've drunk so much at the party you start trying to explain how you'd solve all of the world's problems to anyone who will listen.

When you realise this is your responsibility for the next 18 years.

When you realise you've reached the end of your favourite box set.

When you're fuming because you can't do the metal loop puzzle from your Christmas cracker.

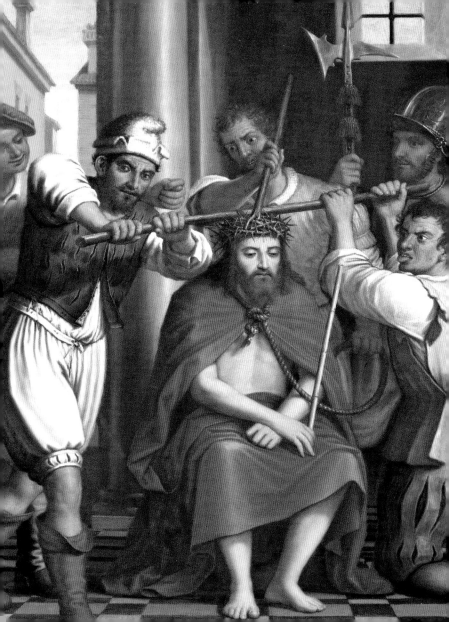

When they want you to join in their game of limbo, but you're really not feeling it.

When you realise you are the most fabulous person in the room.

When you decide to work from home and find out the guy upstairs is learning to play the drums.

When the party-pooper in the room interrupts your 'pull the chair away as they sit down' prank.

*When your crew want to share
your starter, even though
they didn't order their own.*

When you get caught reading your partner's copy of 'Fifty Shades of Grey'.

When, after ignoring his knock at the door, your neighbour appears at the window, insisting you must hear his new violin suite.

When you come up with another devious plan to wake up your parents in the middle of the night.

When you've lost him forever to that home-brewing kit you bought him for Christmas.

When that game of Scrabble™ *should have ended hours ago, but Grandad is still searching the dictionary to prove he has a game winning word.*

When you get nominated for the 'Ice Bucket Challenge', but haven't really got into the spirit of it.

When you think of a great quip to tweet, but it's more than 140 characters.

When you've wasted your whole day putting together a flat-pack desk, only to find the last screw is missing.

When you've had four of your '5 A Day' and now can't even look at another bit of fruit.

When you don't want to look stupid and give someone directions, despite not having any idea where they need to go.

When you can't decide whether to go to the fancy dress party as Jesus or a super hero.